Women in the Bible and What We Can Learn from Them

Monica Roth

TEACH Services, Inc.
PUBLISHING
www.TEACHServices.com • (800) 367-1844

World rights reserved. This book or any portion thereof may not be copied or reproduced in any form or manner whatever, except as provided by law, without the written permission of the publisher, except by a reviewer who may quote brief passages in a review.

The author assumes full responsibility for the accuracy of all facts and quotations as cited in this book. The opinions expressed in this book are the author's personal views and interpretations and do not necessarily reflect those of the publisher.

This book is provided with the understanding that the publisher is not engaged in giving spiritual, legal, medical, or other professional advice. If authoritative advice is needed, the reader should seek the counsel of a competent professional.

Copyright © 2023 Monica Roth
Copyright © 2023 TEACH Services, Inc.
ISBN-13: 978-1-4796-1547-6 (Paperback)
ISBN-13: 978-1-4796-1548-3 (ePub)
Library of Congress Control Number: 2022922645

Unless otherwise noted, all scriptures are taken from the Holy Bible, New King James Version®. Copyright ©1982 by Thomas Nelson. All rights reserved.

A WORD OF PRAISE...

"Monica Roth reminds us that no matter what damaging messages the world sends women, we are valued and cared for by the God of the universe. She brings to life the stories of five Biblical women, drawing thoughtful parallels between their struggles and our lives in the twenty-first century. Every chapter reminded me that God cares about me and what I'm going through. The reflection questions at the end of each chapter have given me a lot to talk to the Lord about in my quiet time with Him. This is a great book for personal study, but it would also work well for a women's book club. If you know a woman who is having a rough time, share this book with her to help her remember that God knows exactly what she's going through and is with her every step of the way."

—Michelle Lashier, Author

"I couldn't put this book down. The chapters are fun and easy to read, with gems of truth I want to remember and apply to my everyday life. This is a great book to have on the shelf and read over and over, to read with others and discuss, and to give as a gift to those you love and care about. Monica's personality shines through as warm, loving, and fun. May you find what you need as you open the pages."

—Holly Lastine, Certified Counselor, Pastor's Wife, and Sabbath School Teacher

"This beautiful devotional is written for women who desire a closer walk with their Savior. It is full of profound insights and relevant applications for our lives. Perfect for individual or group study!"
—Karen Lewis, Ministerial Director for MN Conf.,
Pastor, Pathways Adventist Church

TABLE OF CONTENTS

1	Sarah—God Keeps His Promises and Does the Impossible	9
2	Hagar—God Sees You When You Are Hurting	19
3	Ruth—God Stays	27
4	Mary—God Chooses	39
5	Esther—God Calls and Knows Each One of Us Personally	53

DEDICATION

To my daughters, Angela and Alycia, and every woman, young or old, who needs to be reminded of God's deep love and faithful promises.

ACKNOWLEDGMENTS

Thank you to my editors, Beth Thomas and John Simon, who spent endless hours going through my manuscript. Without Jesus and you, this book would never have been possible.

Many thanks to TEACH Services, Inc. I am so grateful for your amazing team!

Thank you to Lori Roth, who gave of her beautiful artistic talent by painting the cover of this book.

Thank you also to Isaac Conner, for his artistic background color design on the book cover.

Thank you to my son, Nicholas, who encouraged me to persevere while writing this devotional book.

May God bless each and every one of you for being a part of this.

Sarah

CHAPTER 1

SARAH—GOD KEEPS HIS PROMISES AND DOES THE IMPOSSIBLE

Who she was: Abraham's wife
Occupation: Housewife
Status: Wealthy itinerant

Our story today features an episode in the life of Sarai, Abram's wife. Some of Sarai's choices brought pain and guilt—the consequences that sin always brings—but God's love, mercy, and grace reached out to draw her back into the center of His will.

Sarai was a beautiful and wealthy woman. She was so stunning, when their family went to Egypt, Abram feared for his life, believing the Egyptians would become enraptured with her beauty and try to kill him (see Gen. 12:11–14). Abram was very rich in livestock, silver, and gold (see 13:2), but Sarai wanted something looks and money can't buy: a child.

God promised Abram that one day, he would have a son—a biological heir (see 15:4, 5). Sarai

> **❝** Some of Sarai's choices brought pain and guilt—the consequences that sin always brings—but God's love, mercy, and grace reached out to draw her back into the center of His will. **❞**

knew God and expected His promise would be fulfilled. After all, God made the promise Himself. Oh, how she longed for a baby!

As Sarai waited for the promised child, however, she became impatient. The blessing just wasn't coming. Sarai wasn't able to conceive. Exasperated and feeling that perhaps God needed some help, she took matters into her own hands. She took control, made a plan, and stepped outside His will.

Sarai didn't pray and ask God for His guidance, then wait for His direction. She used her beauty, power, and status to take control instead—to get what she wanted, when she wanted it. She decided she would make God's plan come true her own way.

Like Sarai, we all have to wait sometimes for God's promises to be fulfilled. What happens when the waiting gets long and things don't seem to be happening? Will we wait for the very best God has for us or step out of His will and try to do things our own way? We can learn a life lesson from Sarai's decision.

Let's dive into the story: "Now Sarai, Abram's wife, had borne him no *children*. And she had an Egyptian maidservant whose name was Hagar. So Sarai said to Abram, 'See now, the LORD has restrained me from bearing *children*. Please, go in to my maid; perhaps I shall obtain children by her.' And Abram heeded the voice of Sarai" (16:1, 2).

Note that Abram didn't listen to the voice of the Lord; he listened to Sarai and took Hagar as a second wife. Even though it was an acceptable practice in those days for a maidservant to act as a surrogate mother for a mistress who couldn't have her own children (see 30:3), it was not God's plan for Sarai and Abram.

"So he went in to Hagar, and she conceived. And when she saw that she had conceived, her mistress became despised in her eyes" (16:4). In other words, Hagar began treating Sarai with contempt after realizing she was pregnant with Abram's child.

Who did Sarai blame when things turned sour? Herself? No. She blamed her husband. "Then Sarai said to Abram, 'My wrong be upon you!'" (verse 5). Isn't it just like human nature to blame someone else instead of taking responsibility for our own decisions and actions?

Sarai finished by saying, "I gave my maid into your embrace; and when she saw that she conceived, I became despised in her eyes. The LORD judge between you and me." Sarai saw that her action—taking control and forcing "God's" plan—caused a major problem, so she tried to transfer the responsibility to Abram. To her accusation, he replied, "'Indeed your maid is in your hand; do to her as you please.' And when Sarai dealt harshly with her, she fled from her presence" (verse 6).

Hagar despised Sarai. Perhaps she felt resentful because the baby she carried wouldn't be considered her own. Perhaps she felt she deserved a better position in the household as the mother of Abram's child. The Bible doesn't give us those details. Regardless, Sarai dealt harshly with Hagar, and she ran away, taking the longed-for baby with her.

If Sarai had prayed, waiting on God for His direction and trusting Him for His timing and plan, she could've saved Abram, Hagar, and herself so much pain. Sometimes, it is difficult to wait, but stepping out of God's will always leads to unhappiness and inevitable consequences.

As Hagar rested beside a well in the desert, an angel appeared to her, gently chiding her for running from her responsibilities. "The angel of the Lord said to her, 'Return to your mistress, and submit yourself under her hand'" (verse 9). Therefore, Hagar returned to Sarai, eventually gave birth to a son, and named him Ishmael—"God shall hear." Although she went back, the jealousy, broken trust, and hurt feelings caused by Sarai's treatment resulted in a permanent rift in their relationship.

We often make mistakes and try to do things our own way, leaving a trail of pain behind. God, in His rich love, grace, and mercy, can bring good even out of our mistakes. "And we know that all things work together for good to those who love God, to those who are called according to *His* purpose" (Rom. 8:28). God can work miracles; He is in the business of changing our lives for the better!

Watch what God did for Sarai. "Then God said to Abraham, 'As for Sarai your wife, you shall not call her name Sarai, but Sarah shall be her name. And I will bless her and also give you a son by her; then I will bless her, and she shall be a mother of nations; kings of peoples shall be from her'"(Gen. 17:15, 16). As an example of His great love and grace for Sarai, God changed her name to Sarah, confirming He would change her life with the promise He had for her.

God the Father does this for each one of us through Jesus' death on the cross. We are no longer children of the world, for we were purchased by the precious blood of Christ. When we know to whom we belong, we have the assurance that our Father will do more than we can ask or think. He will accomplish the impossible for us.

Let's get back to the story. One afternoon, three travelers stopped at Abraham's campsite in the desert. As they talked, one of the visitors inquired about Abraham's wife. Abraham replied that she was in the tent. "'I will certainly return to you according to the time of life, and behold, Sarah, your wife, shall have a son'" (18:10), the Visitor promised. With that statement, Abraham instantly knew his guests were divine.

God told Abraham Sarah was going to have a son. Sarah, who was listening through the tent door, heard the promise with her own ears. Everything for which she had once hoped would come true! However, she would be ninety years old when she gave birth. As Sarah thought about that, she laughed inwardly. "After I have grown old, shall I have pleasure, my lord being old also?" she said quietly to herself. The heavenly Visitor, knowing all things, heard Sarah's inner laugh. "The Lord said to Abraham, 'Why did Sarah laugh, saying, "Shall I surely bear a child, since I am old?" Is anything too hard for the Lord? At the appointed time I will return to you, according to the time of life, and Sarah shall have a son'" (verses 11–14).

I get why Sarah laughed. If I was going to be ninety years old and heard I was going to have a baby, I'd probably laugh, too! I'd be like, *"What, God? Did I hear you right? You know this is kind of impossible at my age, right?"* God wants us to trust Him—to know He can change the impossible to the possible. God can do mighty things in us and through us as we put our trust and faith in Him. Don't underestimate the power of God and His promises.

Is there an area in your life where God is saying, "This seems impossible, but will you trust me?" It's not always easy to trust when we look at the mountain of challenges to overcome, but Jesus promises, "With men this is impossible, but with God all things are possible" (Matt. 19:26).

Let's trust God and have faith in what He will do—not in our own strength, but in His mighty power. And when we allow God to have ultimate control over our lives, He will do amazing things for us.

God kept His promise just like He said He would, and Sarah gave birth to a son one year later. God is trustworthy! He keeps His promises. He never disappoints. He is always on time and always comes through. Take your eyes off the impossible situation and turn them to God. Let your faith rise, for the God who created the whole world is your Abba Father and will do great things for you and through you.

Others may fail or have failed you, but God is faithful. He never fails. As we look at Sarah's life and see God's grace and goodness towards her, even after her lack of faith, distrust, and manipulation of circumstances, we can trust He will do the same for us.

"And the Lord visited Sarah as He had said, and the Lord did for Sarah as He had spoken" (Gen. 21:1). In order for God's promise to come true, Sarah had to have faith that what He had promised, He would accomplish. Her body was far past the age of childbearing, and she could not trust in her own strength to get the job done. It was that for which God was waiting: her total dependence on Him.

Sarah joins the biblical "Hall of Faith" because of her belief in action. "By faith Sarah herself also received strength to conceive seed, and she bore a child when she was past the age, because she judged Him faithful who had promised" (Heb. 11:11). Sarah had faith in what God had promised her because she knew Him to be faithful. Remember, though, she laughed at first. She questioned God's ability.

God was faithful even though she initially doubted Him! He didn't say, "Oh, because you laughed and doubted me, I won't do this for you." Instead, He asked *why* she doubted, then said, "Is anything too hard for the Lord?" (Gen. 18:14). God gave Sarah something to believe, then built her faith by keeping His promise to her. The combination of her belief in His promise and His miracle-working power gave her body the strength to conceive.

What is it you don't think God is able to do? He will do more than you can ask or think. Ask Him, trust Him, and watch for the miracle He will perform. Sometimes, waiting is hard. The word "wait" often has a negative connotation, but waiting for what God has for you is good. If God is asking you to wait, it means He is getting things ready. When God says wait, He is essentially saying, "I got this. Trust Me. Have faith." Wait with expectancy because we serve a God who does the impossible. As you are waiting, start praising!

Sarah was just an ordinary woman, but the God she knew was extraordinary! He took a woman who was unable to have children and made her the mother of nations. God took her mustard seed of faith and blossomed it. He redeemed and blessed her, not because of her own merit, but because of His own faithfulness. He can do the same for you. Let your faith be in His power and know that what we can't do on our own, God will do for His glory.

Encouraging Promises

"Now faith is the substance of things hoped for, the evidence of things not seen" (Heb. 11:1).

"So Jesus said to them, 'Because of your unbelief; for assuredly, I say to you, if you have faith as a mustard seed, you will say to this mountain, "Move from here to there," and it will move; and nothing will be impossible for you'" (Matt. 17:20).

Relevant Lessons from Sarah's Life

- Ask for God's leading and direction in every major decision.

- Let God's perfect plan unfold in your life as you pray and trust Him for guidance. Wait and stay in God's timing because when you don't, it often causes pain for you and those around you.

- Don't take the control out of God's hands by doing things your own way. It's a dangerous move to step out of His will. Allow the Holy Spirit to give you self-control and let God work.

- You are never too old (or too young) for God to use. If He chose Sarah at ninety years old to become the mother of nations, He can surely use you for mighty things as you put your faith in Him.

- When God speaks, He is faithful to His word.

- Have faith in the God of the impossible. He can do great things in your life as you trust in Him.

Reflection Questions

Is there something for which God is asking you to wait to develop your faith?

Why do you think it is worth waiting for what God has for you?

Is there a Bible verse that has helped you in this study? If so, share it or write it here and ask God to help you memorize it.

What can we learn from Sarah's choice to not wait for God's direction and do things her own way by having a child through Hagar?

What is an acceptable and common practice of our time may not be the best God has for you. Are there areas where you have accepted mankind's ways and ignored God's way? What can you learn from those experiences?

Have you stepped out of God's will? Will you trust Him to fix your life?

Why do you think it is important to take responsibility for your own actions?

Do you think God can use your mistakes for His glory, just like He did for Sarah?

Is there an area in your life of which you are trying to take control but know God wants you to give it to Him? Have faith and watch what He will do as you relinquish the control to Him.

Has there been a time when God worked in a way that helped your faith to grow because you knew it was His divine intervention in your life? If so, write it here to help increase your faith for your present situation or share it to help someone else.

Sarah had faith because she heard the word of God—His promise. Why do you think it is important to read God's Word?

Hagar

CHAPTER 2

HAGAR—GOD SEES YOU WHEN YOU ARE HURTING

Who she was: An Egyptian servant who became Abraham's second wife
Occupation: Sarah's maid
Status: Working class

Hagar's story begins in Genesis 16. She was thrust into a difficult situation—not of her own choice. As you read her story, you will see her struggle as she plays a part in Sarai's plan to have a child.

Abram took Hagar as his second wife, based on Sarai's suggestion. Hagar conceived, and when she realized she was pregnant, she became boastful and treated Sarai with contempt. The Bible says she despised her mistress.

Abram and Sarai met to discuss the problem. "Abram said to Sarai, 'Indeed your maid is in your hand; do to her as you please.' And when Sarai dealt harshly with her, she fled from her presence" (16:6). This was a test. How would Hagar cope? How would she manage this time of deep despair and anguish? There was only One to whom she could turn. In this story, we will explore how God comes through in our greatest times of emotional need.

Like Hagar, people sometimes choose to run away from their problems. However, God knew right where she was going; and He knows right where we are, too. We can never hide from His searching gaze. "For the eyes of the Lord run to and fro throughout the whole earth, to show Himself strong on behalf of *those* whose heart *is* loyal to Him" (2 Chron. 16:9).

In Genesis 16:7, we find Hagar in the desert. "Now the Angel of the Lord found her by a spring of water in the wilderness, by the spring on the way to Shur." She was thirsty, but not just for a drink of fresh spring water. She needed a drink of spiritual water. She needed Jesus.

> "
> Like Hagar, people sometimes choose to run away from their problems. However, God knew right where she was going; and He knows right where we are, too. We can never hide from His searching gaze.
> "

Jesus is that Water of Life. "And the Spirit and the bride say, 'Come!' And let him who hears say, 'Come!' And let him who thirsts come. Whoever desires, let him take the water of life freely" (Rev. 22:17). Jesus invites anyone who hears to come to Him for spiritual life.

When there is nowhere else to turn—nowhere else to run—God has the answer. His life-giving water brings energy to our dry, weary bones. He invites us to come to Him because He knows what we need. He knows that without Him, our lives will be devoid of true life. No one can satisfy our deep longing for love other than God. "If anyone thirst, let him come to Me and drink" (John 7:37). He was the answer for Hagar; and He is the answer for you.

As Hagar sat beside the well in the desert, the Angel asked, "'Hagar, Sarai's maid, where have you come from, and where are you going?' She said, 'I am fleeing from the presence of my mistress Sarai'" (Gen. 16:8). Notice He called her by her name and title: "Hagar, Sarai's maid." He knew everything about her. God knows everything about us, too—exactly where we are and the experiences through which we are going. God knew she was headed in the wrong direction and sent a Messenger to turn her around.

God may not send an angel, but He has sent us the Holy Spirit to impress upon us the way we should go. "For I know the thoughts that I think toward you ... thoughts of peace and not of evil, to give you a future and a hope" (Jer. 29:11). His plans for us are good. He had good in mind for Hagar, but she needed to listen to His instruction.

The Angel said to her, "Return to your mistress, and submit yourself under her hand" (Gen. 16:9). As we learned in verse 6, Sarai dealt harshly with Hagar. It was the reason she fled. I'm sure Hagar was thinking, 'Oh, I don't think so! I'm *not* doing that. That doesn't sound like fun to me.' If she had found the situation with Abram and Sarai enjoyable, she wouldn't have left in the first place. However, the Angel of the Lord instructed her to return. This would be hard. Would she listen to God?

The Angel of the Lord assured her, "I will multiply your descendants exceedingly, so that they shall not be counted for multitude" (verse 10). God knows it isn't always easy to do the right thing. He promised He would help Hagar and bless her for her obedience to Him.

God reminds us, "Fear not, for I am with you; Be not dismayed, for I am your God. I will strengthen you, Yes, I will help you, I will uphold you with My righteous right hand" (Isa. 41:10). In the midst of your wilderness experience, God will find you. He will give you strength to do right.

In the deepest of hurt and the lowest of lows, God is there. He will help you be the woman He is calling you to be and meet you right where you are. He doesn't care what you are wearing or what you look like; He cares deeply about where you are going. Ask Him to show you the way you should go. He directed Hagar; and He will direct you. Hagar's life became more than what she ever imagined as she was obedient to God. She listened, and He blessed her and her son. God will bless you, too, as you follow His will for your life.

Through the Angel, God told Hagar to name her son Ishmael—"God listens." He heard her; He felt her pain. When we think God doesn't see the pain through which we are going, He does. He is there with us, walking with us, and comforting us. He promises us, "Yea, though I walk through the valley of the shadow of death, I will fear no evil: For you are with me; Your rod and Your staff, they comfort me" (Ps. 23:4).

God is with us in our deepest pain, sleepless nights, and through our times of despair. He is the Good Shepherd who cares for us and brings us comfort. When we hurt, He hurts. He promises to comfort us when we mourn, and if you are going through a loss, know that He is right there with you. You might feel at times that no one understands the pain, but God does.

"You number my wanderings; Put my tears into Your bottle; Are they not in Your book?" (Ps. 56:8). His Word reminds us that He sees each tear we cry. In the quiet times of anguish, God has been right there catching each one. He cares for us more deeply than anyone else can.

Hagar referred to God as "You-Are-the-God-Who-Sees; for she said, 'Have I also here seen Him who sees me?'" (Gen. 16:13). Hagar knew it was God who saw her. It was God who met her in her time of despair and anguish. Even though she felt alone, she wasn't. God was right there with her.

If you are struggling, you may be asking, "Where is God in all of this?" Hagar knew she had seen God in her time of anguish. He spoke to her. She saw her Savior's love in action. Let God reveal Himself to you in your hardship. Hagar listened to the Lord and went back. "Hagar bore Abram a son; and Abram named his son, whom Hagar bore, Ishmael" (verse 15).

After a time, Sarah had a son, Isaac. One day, she saw Ishmael mocking Isaac:

> And Sarah saw the son of Hagar the Egyptian, whom she had borne to Abraham, scoffing. Therefore she said to Abraham, "Cast out this bondwoman and her son; for the son of this bondwoman shall not be heir with my son, *namely* with Isaac." … So Abraham rose early in the morning, and took bread and a skin of water; and putting *it* on her shoulder, he gave *it* and the boy to Hagar, and sent her away. Then she departed and wandered in the Wilderness of Beersheba. (Genesis 21:9, 10, 14)

The water was soon gone in the heat of the desert. Hagar, losing hope, placed her son under a shrub to provide some shade, then sat down a little distance away. "She said to herself, 'Let me not see the death of the boy.' So she sat opposite him, and lifted her voice and wept" (verse 16).

At the thought that her son might die, Hagar poured out her heart in deep anguish. "God heard the voice of the lad. Then the Angel of God called to Hagar out of heaven, and said to her, 'What ails you, Hagar? Fear not, for God has heard the voice of the lad where he is'" (verse 17). Our cries do not go unnoticed. God hears us from heaven!

God encouraged Hagar, "Arise, lift up the lad and hold him with your hand, for I will make him a great nation" (verse 18). At her deepest time of despair, He told her not to give up—to stand up and go on. When Hagar felt she couldn't go on, God told her she could. When we are at the end of our rope, God is there! He meets us when we are hurting the most and reaches out to help and heal us. He gives us strength to go on, no matter what we are experiencing. He gives us confidence to get up—to keep going. When we find life most difficult, God gives us the strength to press on.

Hagar knew she had nothing left—no water in her jug. "God opened her eyes, and she saw a well of water. And she went and filled the skin with water, and gave the lad a drink" (verse 19). God will not leave or forsake us; He will provide all we need.

If you need emotional strength, ask God. Trust that He will supply all you need to keep going. He supplied Hagar; and He will supply you. God sees everything through which you are going. He sees every tear and every cry for help. Let Him help and sustain you through your time of despair. Let Him reach into your very soul and heal you of the pain you are experiencing. God is able; He is enough; He will help you.

God promises, "Fear not, for I am with you; Be not dismayed, for I am your God. I will strengthen you, Yes, I will help you, I will uphold you with My righteous right hand" (Isa. 41:10). He will bring you emotional strength in your wilderness. He continues, " I will open rivers in desolate heights, and fountains in the midst of the valleys: I will make the wilderness a pool of water, and the dry land springs of water" (verse 18). God is with us in our valleys, wilderness moments, and times of deepest anguish. He will pull us from the depths of despair and help us stand tall. God will give us the strength to go on.

I found personal encouragement in the story of Hagar as I experienced the loss of my sixteen-month-old grandson, Blake. I felt so alone as I struggled to encourage my grieving daughter while grappling with my own sense of loss. However, the Lord reassured me that He is the God who sees. He saw me at my weakest when I held my little grandson in my arms as he took his last breath. I was not alone. God was right there holding my hand, wrapping His arms around Blake and me. He continues to do that when the memory brings tears to my eyes.

He is the God who cares; He is the God who gives us strength; and He truly is the God who sees.

Relevant Lessons from Hagar's Life

- During trials, loss, or grief, God meets you in your wilderness experience and gives you strength.

- God sees you. You are not alone. He knows everything through which you are going and will never leave or forsake you.

- When you are at your weakest, God will give you strength.

- God's direction is the best for your life. As you take time to listen to Him speak, God will show you the way.

- Sometimes, your way will be hard, but as you listen to God, He will bless you for your obedience to His guidance.

- Arise! Stand up! Go on! God has great plans for You! "For I know the thoughts that I think toward you, says the LORD, thoughts of peace and not of evil, to give you a future and a hope" (Jer. 29:11).

- God sees that through which you are going, even if no one else does. His love will go to the farthest lengths of the wilderness to find you. God knows that from which you are running, where you are, and where you should go. He sees every tear, and His love reaches out to you just like it did to Hagar because He is the God who sees.

Reflection Questions

While Hagar was going through a wilderness experience, she saw God was right there with her. Have you gone through, or are you currently in, a wilderness experience where you have seen God's hand showing you the way?

A wilderness experience is not easy, but did you trust or are you trusting God to give you the strength to move forward?

If you have gone through a wilderness experience, what did you learn?

Did your wilderness experience draw you closer to God?

Why do you think it is important to be obedient to God's Word in times of trial?

To what part of Hagar's story could you relate the most?

Do you think a wilderness experience should cause you to put your trust, faith, and hope in God?

CHAPTER 3

RUTH—GOD STAYS

Who she was: A Moabite immigrant; Naomi's daughter-in-law
Occupation: Barley and wheat gleaner
Status: Working class in Bethlehem, a Palestinian city

The story of Ruth portrays one of the strongest and most beautiful acts of friendship, commitment, and loyalty I've been honored to read in the Bible. It's the kind of friendship that says, "I will stand with you; I will walk with you in your deepest despair. When all others choose to leave, I will go the full journey with you even though I know it will be very difficult and painful—one that will cause me to cry out to the Lord in anguish, cause me to fall to my knees in prayer, and cause me to ponder if I am strong enough. I will leave all my doubt and desires behind; and yes, I will choose to take this journey with you even though you tell me not to do so. I will go with you anyway.

Our story starts with Ruth 1. In the first two verses, we learn that Naomi and her husband Elimelech moved to the country of Moab with their two sons, Mahlon and Chilion. Naomi's life was about to take a dramatic turn.

Elimelech died suddenly, leaving Naomi in a strange country with their two sons. In time, both boys married. "Now they took wives of the women of Moab: the name of the one was Orpah, and the name of the other Ruth. And they dwelt there about ten years" (1:4). Remarkably, Mahlon and Chilion died in Moab, too.

Now Naomi was not only a widow but also suddenly childless. It's hard for many of us to imagine the depth of sorrow she must have experienced. This harsh journey is what led her to change her name to Mara, which means "bitter" or "sorrow." Most people journey through pain like this alone because the walk is difficult, raw, and uncomfortable. Very few friends choose to help shoulder that sort of emotional baggage.

Left destitute with no way to provide for her needs, Naomi decided to return to her hometown in Judah. "Then she arose with her daughters-in-law that she might return from the country of Moab, for she had heard in the country of Moab that the Lord had visited His people by giving them bread" (verse 6). She reasoned that perhaps life would be a bit easier in a familiar place. "Therefore she went out from the place where she was, and her two daughters-in-law with her; and they went on the way to return to the land of Judah" (verse 7).

Although the women began the journey together, Naomi soon told her daughters-in-law to return to their families; she had nothing left to give them or any way to provide for them. And although they wanted to stay with her, she urged them to go back. As she kissed them goodbye, they all wept together. They loved her and wanted to be with her but knew it would be best for them to go home and find other husbands to take care of them.

Both daughters-in-law made a choice: one stayed and one went. Orpah turned back to her family and pagan gods, but Ruth gave up all her own desires: finding a husband, enjoying the comfort of her own family, and financial security. Even though Naomi pleaded with her to go, Ruth made a very unselfish decision.

This is where we begin to see the beautiful heart of Ruth: in her commitment and devotion to her mother-in-law. She had the kind of selfless, sacrificial, unwavering, determined love that stays.

Ruth chose not to worship pagan gods and left her own family. She chose to follow and trust God instead—to leave the rest behind and go with Naomi. She said, "Entreat me not to leave you, *Or to* turn back from following after you; For wherever you go, I will go; And wherever you lodge, I will lodge; Your people *shall be* my people, And your God, my God. Where you die, I will die, And there will I be buried. The LORD do so to me, and more also, if *anything but* death parts you and me" (verses 16, 17).

Sometimes, the journey you walk with someone is difficult and painful. It would be easier to turn back. It's like walking up a hill; but because the love of God compels you, you say, "Yes, I will go with you. I will take off my pretty shoes; I will put on my boots and walk through the trenches with you—not because you want me to, but because the love of God compels me." You say, "Where you go, I will go." That is the love of Christ—the love that says, "I will never leave you or forsake you."

If you choose this kind of love when someone is hurting, it will cause you, like Ruth, to be unselfish. You will need to walk beside that person through the journey of hurt or grief; to listen to and cry with him or her when that person is hurting; to come alongside him or her and say, "I am here for you; I will cry with you; I will take time to listen to and help you; I will not leave you to hurt on your own." This is a beautiful example of God's love.

It reminds me of the story of the good Samaritan. As others chose to pass by when the person was hurting, the hated Samaritan stopped to help. That man—that friend—was the love of Christ in action—the kind who will stop to bandage wounds, no matter what kind they are.

Ruth would not leave Naomi. "Then they lifted up their voices and wept again; and Orpah kissed her mother-in-law, but Ruth clung to her" (verse 14). I'm sure it wasn't easy for Ruth to say, "You're bitter; you're having a difficult time; but I will go with you. I will not let you go alone; I will stay." She chose to travel this difficult path out of love for Naomi, and we will see how God blessed Ruth because of her decision.

Do you have the kind of love that won't let go? the kind of love God wants us to have? the kind of love that comes alongside someone when that person is hurting? The Bible reminds us that love is an action word: "My little children, let us not love in word or in tongue, but in deed and in truth" (1 John 3:18).

At the end of the first chapter, Ruth and Naomi arrived in Bethlehem. Naomi's old neighbors and friends were excited to see her, greeting her by name, but here is where we see her deep pain. She told them to call her Mara, Hebrew for "bitter" or "sorrow." She won't let them call her by her real name, "pleasant," because right now, her life is far from pleasant.

Naomi said, " I went out full, and the Lord has brought me home again empty. Why do you call me Naomi, since the Lord has testified against me, and the Almighty has afflicted me" (Ruth 1:21). However, in verse 22, we see how God cared for them. He brought them back to Bethlehem right at the beginning of the barley harvest. God always has a plan to bring good to His people who love and trust Him. He cares for His own. Let's see the mighty hand of God in His provision for both Ruth and Naomi.

As chapter 2 opens, we see a glimpse of God's plan to provide and care for the two widows. Ruth and Naomi must have felt very alone and afraid at times and in financial need as they came to Bethlehem, both without husbands. They knew they must depend on the Lord. It reminds me of Isaiah 54:4–5, one of my favorite verses in the Bible. These two women learned to know God, not only as their Redeemer and Friend, but also as a Husband who would love and care for them.

In Ruth 2:1, we are introduced to Naomi's husband's distant relative, Boaz, a landowner and man of great wealth. Ruth took it upon herself to see if she could find work, or at least food, with which to support Naomi and herself. Seeing a field close by their home, Ruth asked Naomi if she may go and glean leftover grain. Naomi encouraged her: "Go, my daughter!" The field just happened to belong to Boaz.

Ruth found favor right away with Boaz. He asked his workers who she was, and they told him it was the young Moabite woman who came back with Naomi. Boaz told Ruth to stay with his workers and not glean in another field. He made sure Ruth received sufficient care from his men.

"So she fell on her face, bowed down to the ground, and said to him, 'Why have I found favor in your eyes, that you should take notice of me, since I am a foreigner?'" (verse 10). Ruth knew most people wouldn't even talk to foreigners, let alone show favor to them. "Boaz answered and said to her, 'It has been fully reported to me all that you have done for your mother-in-law since the death of your husband, and how you have left your father and your mother and the land of your birth, and have come to a people whom you did not know before'" (verse 11).

Boaz acknowledged how Ruth left everything she had—her family, home—everything—to help Naomi. He also knew she was trusting God for shelter, security, work, and food. She was trusting God for everything she needed. Boaz said, "The Lord repay your work, and a full reward be given you by the Lord God of Israel, *under whose wings you have come for refuge*" (verse 12, emphasis added).

Boaz invited Ruth to continue working in his fields and eat with his workers at meal time. This she did gratefully and took some home to Naomi. Shocked by the amount of food she was able to save, Naomi asked about her day and which field she gleaned. Ruth told her mother-in-law all about Boaz. Naomi excitedly told her Boaz was a distant relative.

Ruth told Naomi that Boaz told her to stay close to his workers until the end of the harvest. They both believed it was a good plan, and Ruth stayed there until the barley and wheat harvests were finished.

What began as a time of great uncertainty for Ruth and Naomi—in need, with no support or financial security—ended with the assurance that God cared for them and would not leave them alone. He was with them every step of the way.

God provided everything they needed, just when they needed it most. He didn't disappoint them, and He won't disappoint you. He knows exactly what you need. Trust the God who gives—the God who guides—the God who leads and provides for you.

As chapter 3 begins, we see the love Naomi has for Ruth, her daughter-in-law. "*My daughter*, shall I not seek security for you, that it may be well with you?" (verse 1, emphasis added). Notice here that she doesn't call her "daughter-in-law." She says, "my daughter." This love is the type of caring heart a mom might have who wants what's best for her daughter. Ruth had left her family behind, but God had given her a mother through Naomi.

Naomi wanted to provide more for Ruth; she wanted her to find a godly husband; and she had just the man in mind: Boaz. Naomi gave Ruth some interesting instructions, to say the least, and Ruth listened. She trusted Naomi and knew she loved her and wanted what was best for her. "Listen to counsel and receive instruction, that you may be wise in your latter days" (Prov. 19:20).

We find Naomi's advice to be interesting. She told Ruth that Boaz was at the threshing floor working and would be there that evening.

> "Therefore, wash yourself and anoint yourself, put on your best garment and go down to the threshing floor; but do not make yourself known to the man until he has finished eating and drinking. Then

it shall be, when he lies down, that you shall notice the place where he lies; and you shall go in, uncover his feet, and lie down; and he will tell you what you should do." And she said to her, "All that you say to me I will do." (Ruth 3:3–5)

Naomi knew Israelite law stated that because Boaz was her relative, he could be a kinsman-redeemer and care for Ruth by marrying her. It was not uncommon for a servant to lie at the master's feet at night to stay warm and share covering. It may have been a common practice, but for Ruth to do it must have taken a large amount of courage. She was not afraid to take a risk, for she trusted Naomi.

Now, I'm all about being a bold and courageous woman, but this would have been out of my comfort zone. Go, Ruth! Watch what happens: "And after Boaz had eaten and drunk, and his heart was cheerful, he went to lie down at the end of the heap of grain; and she came in softly, uncovered his feet, and lay down. Now it happened at midnight that the man was startled, and turned himself; and there, a woman was lying at his feet" (verses 7, 8).

Shocked, Boaz asked, "Who are you?" (verse 9).

She replied, "I am Ruth, your maidservant. Take your maidservant under your wing, for you are a close relative." Ruth was so bold as to ask Boaz to keep the Israelite law. You just have to love her boldness. I sure do. She basically says, "Hey, marry me!"

Boaz said, " Blessed are you of the Lord, my daughter! For you have shown more kindness at the end than at the beginning, in that you did not go after young men, whether poor or rich" (verse 10). He knew Ruth could have gone after anyone she wanted, but she didn't. She waited. Ruth didn't turn back to the pagan gods or men with pagan beliefs, and now she is getting to know a man with godly characteristics.

God restored everything to Ruth that she was willing to give up. If you are single, wait until He brings you a Christian man with Christian character. God planned more for Ruth's life than she ever realized, and He was able to bless her because she chose Him first. God has a plan for you, too, so wait until He brings the best.

Boaz told Ruth, "Now it is true that I am a close relative; however, there is a relative closer than I. Stay this night, and in the morning it shall be that if he will perform the duty of a close relative for you, good;

let him do it. But if he does not want to perform the duty for you, then I will perform the duty for you, as the Lord lives! Lie down until morning" (verses 12, 13).

Boaz gave Ruth his word but kept the law by letting the closer relative take his rightful opportunity to perform the law of the kinsman-redeemer first. Boaz walked with integrity and was going to make sure Ruth would have a kinsman-redeemer. She laid at his feet until morning, and we understand from the biblical record that this was a very pure night with no sexual encounter.

> God restored everything to Ruth that she was willing to give up. If you are single, wait until He brings you a Christian man with Christian character. God planned more for Ruth's life than she ever realized, and He was able to bless her because she chose Him first. God has a plan for you, too, so wait until He brings the best.

When Ruth returned home, she was given more instructions. Naomi said, "Sit still, my daughter, until you know how the matter will turn out; for the man will not rest until he has concluded the matter this day" (verse 18). She gave this advice because Boaz would keep his word and not rest until he did so that very day. Naomi was right. Boaz kept his word.

As we conclude chapter 3, we see God's faithfulness and continued care for these two women. We also get a deeper sense of the love, commitment, and trust in Ruth and Naomi's relationship. Ruth listened to wise Naomi's godly advice; Naomi's love was so unselfish that even though Ruth was all she had, she still wanted her to fall in love and get married. They wanted the best for each other. This is a relationship founded on selfless love, trust, loyalty, and commitment. This kind of friendship is a gift far beyond anything money can buy.

This is what God wants for you; He is committed to you. **God's love is a love that stays**. His love will never leave you or forsake you. Nothing will separate you from the love God has for you. "For I am persuaded that neither death nor life, nor angels nor principalities nor powers, nor things present nor things to come, nor height nor depth, nor any other created thing, shall be able to separate us from the love of God which is in Christ Jesus our Lord" (Rom. 8:38, 39).

Chapter 4 opens our hearts and minds to see God's love through the parallel of Boaz's love for Ruth as he keeps the Israelite law. This points to the love that prompted God to send Jesus to this earth.

Boaz gathered the elders together to settle the matter, just as Naomi told Ruth he would. "Then he said to the close relative, 'Naomi, who has come back from the country of Moab, sold a piece of land which belonged to our brother Elimelech'" (4:3).

Here we learn that Naomi had sold the land. I'm sure this was out of her need to survive, but now Boaz is going to try to buy it back. The story continues: "Then Boaz said, 'On the day you buy the field from the hand of Naomi, you must also buy it from Ruth the Moabitess, the wife of the dead, to perpetuate the name of the dead through his inheritance'" (verse 5).

The other relative didn't want to perform his responsibility, so he gave Boaz the opportunity to buy the land—and win Ruth.

> Boaz said to the elders and all the people, "You are witnesses this day that I have bought all that was Elimelech's, and all that was Chilion's and Mahlon's, from the hand of Naomi. Moreover, Ruth the Moabitess, the widow of Mahlon, I have acquired as my wife, to perpetuate the name of the dead through his inheritance, that the name of the dead may not be cut off from among his brethren and from his position at the gate. You are witnesses this day." (Ruth 4:9, 10)

Boaz exercised the right of the kinsman-redeemer, bought back the land, and kept the law of the brother to take the widow as his wife, care for her, and love her. "So Boaz took Ruth and she became his wife; and when he went into her, the Lord gave her conception, and she bore a son" (verse 13). God blessed Ruth and Boaz for their commitment to Him and each other and the kindness they showed others.

God didn't forget Naomi and her love for Him, either. Sometimes, life is hard, and we, like Naomi, would prefer to stay bitter or sorrowful after the pain. However, God can take even these times and bring good out of them. Naomi's painful experiences ended in joy as God blessed her with a grandson through Ruth.

Naomi's friends even reminded her of how good God was to give her this little blessing: "Then the women said to Naomi, 'Blessed be the Lord, who has not left you this day without a close relative; and may his name be famous in Israel! And may he be to you a restorer of life and a nourisher of your old age; for your daughter-in-law, who loves you, who is better to you than seven sons, has borne him'" (verses 14, 15).

Ruth and Boaz named their son Obed. He was the father of Jesse, the father of David. This child is in the genealogy of Jesus. Ruth received back from the Lord everything she was willing to give up. She receives a husband, financial security, and a baby boy who is in the line of our Savior!

Boaz is a beautiful parallel to Jesus. He provided food to satisfy Ruth and Naomi's physical needs and a warm covering for Ruth on that cold harvest night. He covered her with his love when she became his bride and promised to care for her for the rest of her life.

Jesus is our Redeemer! He buys us back. His death on the cross enabled our inheritance of eternal life. We need a redeemer, just as Naomi did. We once sold our land—our lives—to the power of the enemy, but God, in His love, kindness, and mercy, bought us back.

God gave Jesus the right to take the power of sin and death and crucify it. He sent His son to die on the cross and take our place for sin. Jesus takes back our lives from the enemy's power. God's love redeems you, restores you, and calls you His own. He has cleansed you by His blood. He has placed you in right standing before God.

"If you confess with your mouth the Lord Jesus and believe in your heart that God has raised Him from the dead, you will be saved" (Rom. 10:9). If you have never prayed this prayer to receive the free gift of eternal life, I encourage you to do so now.

Sisters in the Lord, know the love of Christ, the One who went the long journey to Calvary for you; the One who paid the price to redeem you; the One who gave up His heavenly home to lay down His life for you so you can have the inheritance of eternal life. You are covered with His love through the blood He shed on the cross. Jesus calls you His own because He paid the price through His deep love for you. He has redeemed you. He says, "You are mine! You are My child—My daughter!"

God's love will never let go. It clings to you like Ruth clung to Naomi. It will never leave you. His love goes through the darkest, hardest times because He is the God who stays.

Relevant Lessons from Ruth's Life

- God's love goes the distance. Ruth was willing to walk with Naomi even through the hardest season of her life. Ruth was committed, loyal, and determined to stay, even when no one else would.

- God provided for Ruth and Naomi in ways they could never have imagined. He came through every step of the way. Ruth had no inkling of the plans God had for her future, but He provided everything she needed. At times of uncertainty, God always comes through.

- **Listening to godly advice is rewarding.** Naomi gave Ruth instructions, and Ruth wisely listened. She was blessed each time she listened and followed through.

- Ruth was willing to leave her desires and old life behind as she chose God. She made the decision to stay with Naomi, and God returned to her everything she was willing to give up and more than she could have ever imagined. He gave Ruth a godly husband who loved her with a divine brand of love. And most of all, Ruth and Boaz were blessed with a son who was in the genealogy of Jesus.

Reflection Questions

Is God asking you to be a Ruth in someone's life who is going through a difficult time? Are you willing?

In the story of the good Samaritan, are you the priest, Levite, or Samaritan? (see Luke 10:30–37)

Has there been a time in your life when you were in financial need and saw the hand of God provide for you? It is important to remember these times because it gives us faith to trust Him when we are in need.

If you are single and desire to be married, can you see how God blessed Ruth with a man of integrity as she put Him first in her life?

Why do you think Boaz called Ruth a virtuous woman?

What kind of love inspired Ruth to go the long journey with Naomi?

Do you know Jesus as your personal Redeemer? Have you accepted the price He paid to redeem you? His love reaches out to you.

CHAPTER 4

MARY—GOD CHOOSES

Who she was: A Jewish virgin, betrothed to Joseph
Occupation: A peasant who became the mother of Jesus
Status: Working class in Nazareth, a city in Galilee
This story is found in Matthew 1:18–25 and Luke 1:26–56.

Who was Mary? What kind of heart did she have for God to choose her to be the mother of Jesus? In this chapter, we will see a young woman who loved God and gave Him first place in her life. We will see how Mary was willing to give up her hopes and dreams because of her love for God and how she knew there was no greater purpose in life than that which He had for her.

Mary knew that in God's will, she would be blessed. Her love and faith in God is what made it possible for her to say, "Behold the maidservant of the Lord! Let it be to me according to your word" (Luke 1:38).

Our story begins in the tiny village of Nazareth in Galilee. The population was fewer than 400 people, and most of the villagers were farmers. Their daily work consisted of growing crops and raising farm animals for food and clothing. We don't know much about Mary's upbringing or family, but we do know she was betrothed to a man named Joseph.

In Bible times, betrothal was very significant. Many families would come together and promise their children to each other while they were still quite young. When they entered puberty, they would officially become betrothed or engaged. This engagement usually lasted a year, during which the two fiancées lived with their respective families yet were completely committed to each other. The only options that could break this binding agreement was either a written letter of divorce or death. If either party broke the betrothal/engagement by being with another person, he or she could be divorced or, even worse, stoned to death.

During the preparation time, the groom would prepare a home for the couple, usually under his father's supervision, and the bride would spend time sewing or weaving linens and other things for their home together.[1]

The Jewish wedding was more of a feast—a celebration that often lasted for five-to-seven days. On the first day, the groom traveled to the bride's father's house to get his bride. The second day was a grand party with lively singing and gifts, followed by an evening wedding supper. That night, the groom took his bride to their home to consummate the marriage. The feast continued for several days with the bride and groom celebrating with all their guests.

Mary's situation was slightly different, as Joseph was older and already had a family. Still, I'm sure she looked forward to the time when she would have her own home, children, and a strong, faithful husband to love and care for her.

As the day of her wedding approached, Mary must've been excited to have all of her friends and family together, celebrating such a special event. She might've been nervous and even a little bit shy as she thought of the night where she and Joseph would express their love physically to one another for the first time.

As Mary waited for her wedding celebration, a bigger, more glorious plan was unfolding—one far superior to any a young peasant girl could even imagine or expect.

Mary knew God's Word. She heard the Torah (the five books of Moses) read each Sabbath. She knew God had promised a Messiah: "Therefore the Lord Himself will give you a sign: Behold, the virgin shall conceive and bear a Son, and shall call His name Immanuel" (Isa. 7:14).

---

[1] See Theresa Lisiecki, "First Century Jewish Wedding Practices," Saint Colette Catholic Church, https://1ref.us/22e (accessed September 1, 2022).

One day, as Mary was busy with her daily chores, the angel Gabriel appeared to her. Let's pick up the story:

> Now in the sixth month the angel Gabriel was sent by God to a city of Galilee named Nazareth, to a virgin betrothed to a man whose name was Joseph, of the house of David. The virgin's name *was* Mary. And having come in, the angel said to her, "Rejoice, highly favored *one*, the Lord *is* with you; blessed *are* you among women!" But when she saw *him*, she was troubled at his saying, and considered what manner of greeting this was. Then the angel said to her, "Do not be afraid, Mary, for you have found favor with God. And behold, you will conceive in your womb and bring forth a Son, and shall call His name JESUS. He will be great, and will be called the Son of the Highest; and the Lord God will give Him the throne of His father David. And He will reign over the house of Jacob forever, and of His kingdom there will be no end." Then Mary said to the angel, "How can this be, since I do not know a man?" And the angel answered and said to her, "*The* Holy Spirit will come upon you, and the power of the Highest will overshadow you; therefore, also, that Holy One who is to be born will be called the Son of God." (Luke 1:26–35)

As Mary mulled over the angel's words, she thought of Joseph. If he didn't believe her story of how she conceived, her betrothal/engagement, and possibly her life, would be over. However, her faith and trust in God compelled her to say, "Behold the maidservant of the Lord! Let it be to me according to your word" (verse 38). Then Gabriel departed.

God had first place in Mary's heart, and she trusted Him with her life. Because of this, she said yes to God and called herself His maidservant. Mary's desire was to do God's will. God knew this before He even sent the angel to her. He knew He had first place in Mary's heart and soul, and this is what made it possible for Him to take control of every aspect of her life.

In the biggest moment of her life, Mary didn't hesitate when God asked her. She didn't give all the reasons why she couldn't. She didn't ask God to wait until after her wedding day. "You shall love the Lord your God with all your heart, with all your soul; and with all your strength"

(Deut. 6:5). Mary was no doubt familiar with this passage. "With all [her] heart" meant God had her hopes, dreams, and desires. Mary loved God above all else! He had every part of her heart, including her will. She trusted that God was able to take care of every matter that concerned her, and He didn't disappoint.

The moment Mary trusted God and gave Him her future is when her life really began. And God gave her so much more than she planned. Mary knew nothing was better than being in His will. She didn't ask God, "Why?" She didn't give all the reasons why she couldn't. When faced with a major decision, a thousand thoughts go quickly through one's mind. I'm sure Mary was no different, but her answer was "Yes."

Look how God cared for Mary when she told Joseph she was impregnated by the Holy Spirit. Joseph didn't believe her at first. How could he? Therefore, God sent an angel to tell Joseph it was true.

> Now the birth of Jesus Christ was as follows: After His mother Mary was betrothed to Joseph, before they came together, she was found with child of the Holy Spirit. Then Joseph, her husband, being a just man, and not wanting to make her a public example, was minded to put her away secretly. But while he thought about these things, behold, an angel of the Lord appeared to him in a dream, saying, "Joseph, son of David, do not be afraid to take Mary your wife, for that which is conceived in her is of the Holy Spirit. And she will bring forth a Son, and you shall call His name Jesus, for He will save His people from their sins." So all this was done that it might be fulfilled which was spoken by the Lord through the prophet, saying: "Behold, the virgin shall be with child, and bear a Son, and they shall call His name Immanuel, which is translated, 'God with us.'" Then Joseph, being aroused from sleep, did as the angel of the Lord commanded him and took to him his wife, and did not know her till she had brought forth her firstborn Son. And he called His name Jesus. (Matthew 1:18–25)

God took care of every detail of Mary's life. She was willing to give up her plans for His plans and was incredibly blessed for it. God had so much more for Mary then what she was planning. He had a greater purpose for her life.

Sometimes, we hold on to our own plans, but God wants to give us so much more. Are you willing to give up your plans and trust what God has in store for you? Are you able to, like Mary did, trust that God has the very best plan for your life?

I can't imagine a greater calling on a woman's life than to be chosen by God to carry Jesus, the Savior of all mankind. God could have chosen anyone, but He chose humble Mary. As we learn about the heart of Mary and who she was, we see why God chose her.

Mary said, "For He has regarded the lowly state of His maidservant; For behold, henceforth all generations will call me blessed" (Luke 1:48; see verses 46–55). She knew it wasn't because of her greatness that they would call her blessed, but because of the greatness of God. This was His doing, not hers. She knew she was nothing in and of herself or in the world's eyes; therefore, pride couldn't get in the way.

> God resists the proud, but gives grace to the humble. Therefore humble yourselves under the mighty hand of God, that He may exalt you in due time. (1 Peter 5:5, 6)

> If anyone thinks he is something when he is nothing, he deceives himself. (Galatians 6:3, NIV)

Mary was not deceived; she knew she had no great spiritual or economic status. She delivered Jesus and knew He would deliver her from eternal death. She knew she needed a Savior, just like you and I do. "For all have sinned and fall short of the glory of God, being justified freely by His grace through the redemption that is in Christ Jesus" (Rom. 3:23, 24).

Mary knew the Bible prophesied of the Savior who would come and redeem us from sin, and she needed a Savior, too. God's word—the plan for redemption—was being fulfilled as she said "Yes" to Him. Her answer shows she understood this responsibility: "Behold the maidservant of the Lord! Let it be to me according to your word."

Mary's life story is one of the greatest rags-to-riches stories ever—not the riches of the world, but God's riches. She was given a very high honor to be chosen by God to be the mother of Jesus, but her pride never got in the way. She stayed humble.

When it came time to give birth to Jesus, Mary didn't demand the best birthing suite—she was giving birth to the King of kings, after all.

She could have asked for the best place to give birth to Jesus, but she didn't. Jesus was born in one of the humblest places of all: a stable.

God knew the woman He chose would have to rely on Him for strength, and Mary did. Mary trusted God, and her strength and confidence were rooted in Him. God knew Mary would have to withstand gossip and insults in Nazareth. In a small town, everyone knows everyone and everything. Everyone would know Mary told Joseph she was impregnated by the Holy Spirit. If *Joseph* needed an angel of God to explain the story, I'm sure the women in the town wouldn't believe her story either.

As Mary walked through the city to get her water from the well, I'm sure she heard the whispers and saw the judgmental looks. God gave her the strength to face the rejection and condemnation she felt on every side. What was most important to Mary was what God thought of her.

> As Mary walked through the city to get her water from the well, I'm sure she heard the whispers and saw the judgmental looks. God gave her the strength to face the rejection and condemnation she felt on every side. What was most important to Mary was what God thought of her.

Can you say you are like Mary? If God is calling you to do something, are you more concerned about what others may say or think, or is the only thing that matters is what God thinks of you? Have faith like Mary did and see what God can do through you! Do it for His glory.

As Jesus grew, Mary taught Him in the ways of God. She faithfully instructed Him in the Scriptures, knowing they would make Him wise. She helped Him, through the Word, to understand His role in the plan of salvation.

If you have children, you are called to be a mom. Whether you planned the birth of your children or not, the Bible says you are blessed. "Behold, children are a heritage [gift] from the Lord, the fruit of the womb is a reward" (Ps. 127:3, emphasis added). I also think of the great responsibility each one of us has as a mom. It is not an easy task, but it gives great rewards—rewards far greater than anything else you will do in life. If you have children, you are called by the Lord to raise them in His ways.

God gives us instructions to teach our children His Word and commandments: "You shall teach them to your children, speaking of them when you sit in your house, when you walk by the way, when you lie down, and when you rise up" (Deut. 11:19). This is the job God has given us as moms. He promises if we love Him and teach our children to love Him and keep His commandments, He will bless us and our children.

Mary was an example of how each one of us should raise our children up in the ways of the Lord. "And the Child grew and became strong in spirit, filled with wisdom; and the grace of God was upon Him" (Luke 2:40). Mary must have been doing her job as a godly mom, and God's spirit was upon Jesus as He grew.

If God has entrusted you with children, you have the same responsibility He gave Mary: to raise them up in the ways of the Lord. What an honor, privilege, and responsibility God has given to us as moms and, in many cases, grandmothers!

All of our walks are not the same. I don't know what you are experiencing, but I do know God will help you and give you the strength you need. Don't look to your own wisdom and strength, but ask God for direction and help to raise the child(ren) He has given you.

> I will lift up my eyes to the hills—From whence comes my help? My help *comes* from the LORD, Who made heaven and earth. (Psalm 121:1)

> For You formed my inward parts; Your covered me in my mother's womb. (Psalm 139:13)

If God made us and each one of our children, He has the best blueprints and directions for how to raise us *and* our children. Remember, no two are the same, so ask God for directions and wisdom. "If any of you lacks wisdom, let him ask God, who gives to all liberally and without reproach, and it will be given to him" (James 1:5).

Being a mom is not easy, so don't try to do it on your own. Raising children takes a lot of wisdom and hard work. God promises to give us what we need, and if we read His Word, we will find the best instructions on how to raise the children He has given us.

Maybe you're saying, "I've made mistakes as a mom!" Mary did, too. We learn that after Mary and Joseph attended the yearly Passover in Jerusalem, they left to return home to Nazareth. They traveled a whole day before realizing Jesus was not with them. They had to return to Jerusalem. It was three whole days before they found Him in the temple (see Luke 2:40–46).

What was Mary doing? Did she have a thousand things on her mind? Was she stressed out or preoccupied with other things? Whatever the reason, God gave Mary grace and helped her find Jesus.

God could have said, "Really, Mary? I gave you the responsibility to raise My only Son, and you left Him in Jerusalem. You traveled a whole day without Him!" God could have taken Jesus from her and found Him a new mom, but He didn't. What did God do instead? He helped Mary find Jesus.

God knows we are not perfect. No mother is—not even Mary. However, God chose her to be Jesus' mother; and He has chosen us to be mothers, with all our imperfections. God's grace and love will help you raise the child(ren) He has given you. Don't condemn yourself for your mistakes, for God doesn't. Let go of whatever mistakes you have made because God has let them go and keeps no record of wrongs. Trust Him for sufficient strength for today. Yesterday is behind you; today is the day God has given you.

As Mary continued to find her strength and confidence in God, He helped her throughout her life. The pain she endured must have been almost more than she could bear as she watched her Son be crucified. As a mother, there is no greater pain than to lose a child. By this time, Mary was a widow and single parent and suffered Jesus' death alone. Nevertheless, God gave her the grace and strength she needed.

For whatever reason, some are left to raise children as single parents. Even if you are married, at times, you may feel like a single parent. Remember, God sees the needs you have. Just as Jesus made sure His beloved disciple brought Mary in and cared for her, so will He care for you. I believe Jesus has the same love for all mothers that He had for His own mom. Don't try to do this on your own. Ask God for help.

Sometimes, life is hard! Will you trust God to give you the strength for whatever it is you are experiencing? He will give you the strength to make it through. Remember God's promise: "Fear not, for I am with you; Be not dismayed, for I am your God. I will strengthen you, Yes, I will help you, I will uphold you with My righteous right hand"

(Isa. 41:10). God loves you and promises to help you through all hardships. He will never leave you or forsake you. He is right by your side. Allow God to give you the strength to make it through the darkest times in your life. There is no greater strength than His.

Take time to pray and intercede for your children. I wonder how many children have been saved by a mother on her knees. The battle is won when we pray! Mary was a woman of prayer. She prayed in supplication to God alone. "These all continued with one accord in prayer and supplication, with the women and Mary, the mother of Jesus, and with His brothers" (Acts 1:14).

Mary was in the upper room praying to God and interceding for others. Let us mimic her example and pray to our heavenly Father. There is power in prayer! I believe it is the best course of action a mom can take.

Mary needed the strength of God to make it through the deepest loss in her life. She never went on alone; she went on with God by the power of the Holy Spirit. Mary was there at Pentecost when the Holy Spirit came upon them. "But you shall receive power when the Holy Spirit has come upon you" (verse 8), so Mary went on with the power of the Holy Spirit.

The Greek word for "power" in Acts 1:8 is *dunamis*. This is from where our English word "dynamite" comes. God gave Mary dynamite power to go on—the strength to endure. He was with her through it all. She waited in the upper room as Jesus had instructed them to do. Mary knew it would only be through God's strength that she could go on.

Is God asking you to wait in the upper room? Do you need strength from on high? Wait upon the Lord. Spend time praying and asking God to give you strength. He will give you that dynamite power to do whatever He is calling you to do. Look to God, who will empower you. Mary listened to God as she waited in the upper room, and He empowered her.

God has a plan and purpose for your life. There is no greater joy than being in the center of His will. Remember, though, being in God's will is not always easy. It wasn't for Mary, but she went on, knowing He was with her through the Holy Spirit. Mary had hope that she would see Jesus again. She knew the resurrection power of God; He raised Jesus from the dead, and someday, Jesus would return for His mom.

You may have lost a child, husband, or someone close to you. Whatever your loss, let God comfort you. Mary lost both, but God reached His hand out to her and gave her comfort. He is reaching His hand out to you to bring you comfort, too. God cares when we are hurting. "The Lord is near to those who have a broken heart, And saves such as have a contrite spirit" (Ps. 34:18).

What hope and reassurance this must have given Mary! She went on knowing she would see Jesus again because He would return. God gives this same hope to each one of us through Christ.

Mary loved and served God with all her heart and soul. Her love for Him was shown throughout her life. God had first place in Mary's heart. She walked with Him, and as she gave Him her dreams, hopes, and desires, He was able to fulfill the purpose He had for her life.

> Maybe you are thinking, 'I really don't have much to offer God.' Well, Mary didn't, either, but He had her heart, love, trust, and devotion. Mary was a humble woman who knew there was no greatness in and of herself. This is the kind of woman the Lord chooses: a woman who knows she is nothing inherently but recognizes the greatness of the God she serves.

Maybe you are thinking, 'I really don't have much to offer God.' Well, Mary didn't, either, but He had her heart, love, trust, and devotion. Mary was a humble woman who knew there was no greatness in and of herself. This is the kind of woman the Lord chooses: a woman who knows she is nothing inherently but recognizes the greatness of the God she serves.

"Oh, taste and see that the Lord is good; Blessed is the woman who trusts in Him!" (Ps. 34:8).

Relevant Lessons from Mary's Life

- Mary's heart belonged to God. He had first place in her heart. **God wants first place in our hearts.** "Nevertheless I have this against you, that you have left your first love" (Rev. 2:4).

- "You shall love the Lord your God with all your heart, with all your soul, and with all your strength" (Deut. 6:5).

- **Believe God's Word and power.** "For with God nothing will be impossible" (Luke 1:37).

- Mary believed the impossible was possible with God and saw His power work in her life because of it.

- **Raise your children to know God's commandments and Word.** Mary was faithful to the calling God had given her while she raised Jesus. "You shall teach them to your children, speaking of them when you sit in your house, when you walk by the way, when you lie down, and when you rise up" (Deut. 11:19).

- **Be humble.** Give God the glory. Don't let pride take root. There is no room for pride when we remember it is the work of God. "He has put down the mighty from their thrones, and exalted the lowly" (Luke 1:52). "God resists the proud, but gives grace to the humble. Therefore humble yourself under the mighty hand of God, that He may exalt you in due time" (1 Peter 5:5, 6).

- **Trust the Lord.** Will you choose to trust Him? God wants good for us, but we must choose to trust Him and His divine purpose for our lives. What it must have taken Mary to say, "Behold the maidservant of the Lord! Let it be to me according to your word" (Luke 1:38)!

- "Trust the Lord with all your heart, And lean not on your own understanding; in all your ways, acknowledge Him, and He shall direct your paths" (Prov. 3:5, 6).

Reflection Questions

When blessings come in your life, do you give God the glory and praise?

If you have children, do you see them as blessings from the Lord?

Do you spend time teaching your children/grandchildren to love the Lord and keep His Word?

Do you know God in such a personal way that you could say, "God, my Savior" as Mary did?

Who or what has first place in your heart?

Why do you think loving God first is so important?

Are you devoted enough to the Lord to call yourself His maidservant?

Do you trust that God has the very best plan for your life and will work out all the details like He did for Mary?

Are you willing to let God use your life and give you the best He has for you?

Suggested Prayer: Lord, have my heart, that I would humbly serve and trust You in all You ask me to do. In Jesus name, Amen.

CHAPTER 5

ESTHER—GOD CALLS AND KNOWS EACH ONE OF US PERSONALLY

Who she was: A young Jewish woman
Occupation: An involuntary queen
Status: Orphan raised by a cousin who worked in the Persian palace

Have you ever wanted to be royalty? Who doesn't want to be a queen or princess? Maybe you didn't want to be queen, but you daydreamed of wearing a beautiful ball gown and gorgeous crown with jewels that sparkled and gleamed. Today, we are going to take a closer look at Esther, the involuntary queen.

Have you ever been placed in a position and thought, 'I'm in way over my head. I can't even imagine how to accomplish what I'm being asked to do!' Esther was put in a similar position—chosen to accomplish what seemed to be an impossible task.

Esther is between Nehemiah and Job, and our story begins in the first chapter. King Ahasuerus, the Persian ruler, had thrown a lavish party for his governors and princes. In a drunken stupor, he called for Queen Vashti, who was quite beautiful, to come to the banquet so he could show her off. She refused. King Ahasuerus' pride was hurt, and his counselors advised him to immediately remove Queen Vashti and install a new queen. A royal notice was sent out to the entire kingdom, calling all attractive, young, unmarried women to come to the palace. They would provide a pool from which the king could choose a new bride.

Esther was one such woman. After her parents died, Esther was raised by her cousin Mordecai. Having experienced pain and loss at such a young age, her heart had been tried and tested before she even got to the king's palace. She must have had to go through many days of hurt, pain, and trials, but God used these times to make her stronger by teaching her to depend on Him. This type of character is only built through times of testing and adversity. God knew Esther would need this strength when she became queen and changed the history of the Jewish nation.

God uses trials to refine and purify us. We are reminded that He "will bring the *one*-third through the fire, will refine them as silver is refined, and test them as gold is tested. They will call on My name, and I will answer them. I will say, 'This *is* My people'; And each one will say, 'The Lord is my God'" (Zech. 13:9).

Even after Esther became queen, she went through a time of testing, when she, too, had to call upon the Lord for help. So many times, we think things should come fast and easy, but before God can use us for His work, there is a time of preparation. Esther went through a time of preparation, too.

> **"**
> So many times, we think things should come fast and easy, but before God can use us for His work, there is a time of preparation. Esther went through a time of preparation, too.
> **"**

"Each young woman's turn came to go in to King Ahasuerus after she had completed twelve months' preparation, according to the regulations for the women, for thus were the days of their preparation appointed: six months with oil of myrrh, and six months with perfumes and preparations for beautifying women" (Esther 2:12).

Wow! If it took a beautiful young woman that long to get ready to become a queen, I wonder how long it would take me to get ready. As stated before, so many times, we think things should come to us so quickly, but in this verse, I'm reminded that when God is doing a good work in developing our character, it takes longer than we think it should.

I associate the oil with the Holy Spirit, and the perfumes are used to get rid of all my ugly, stinky attitudes. I see why preparation time in some of us, like myself, takes a little longer. Some of us take longer to even get ready to go outside the house, let alone to be ready to be used for God's glory. It's a good thing God is a master at what He does, right, ladies? I'm so thankful He is patient with me even when I'm having a hard time being patient with myself.

Esther found favor within the king's palace right away during her year of preparation. It says she was moved to one of the best places in the house and given seven choice maidservants. God had his hand on her even from the beginning of her time in the palace. God knew the calling He had for Esther to become queen even before she did. He sees you as who He created you to be, even before you are able to fulfill it. Esther may have not been able to see herself as queen, but God did. He paved the way for her.

Now, Esther was young yet wise. She showed this wisdom by listening—listening to her cousin Mordecai and the advice of the king's eunuch. Before she went to the palace, Mordecai cautioned her not to reveal to anyone that she was a Jew. She carefully kept the secret to herself. Before her turn to meet the king, she asked his assistant what she should wear and say. "And Esther obtained favor in the sight of all who saw her" (verse 10).

Listening to advise and godly instruction will help us in life. "The way of a fool is right in his own eyes, But he who heeds counsel is wise" (Prov. 12:15). Esther's choice to follow wise counsel resulted in her becoming queen. "The king loved Esther more than all the other women, and she obtained grace and favor in his sight more than all the virgins; so he set the royal crown upon her head and made her queen instead of Vashti" (Esther 2:17). God was in control.

Esther continued to keep Mordecai's instructions to not reveal she was Jewish. Sometimes, it is hard to listen to advice. We want to do it our own way and don't realize the importance of listening to godly advice or instruction. As we press on in our study, we will see the importance of this and how God saved Esther, as well as many others, because she obeyed.

Now in modern-day stories, when there is a king and queen, there is often an evil or wicked character. This story is no different. Enter Haman. He was second in command to the Ahasuerus, and all the king's servants bowed to him as he had commanded. Mordecai refused, which made Haman quite angry. "When Haman saw that Mordecai did not bow or pay him homage [as the king's law had mandated], Haman was filled with wrath" (3:5)

Mordecai had revealed he was a Jew, so evil Haman set up a dastardly plan against not only Mordecai but all the Jews throughout the whole kingdom. He took his plan to King Ahasuerus. He told the king not all of his subjects were keeping the law and requested that a decree be written to destroy all the Jews—an effort he would personally fund with 10,000 talents of silver.

King Ahasuerus agreed to the plan, but what he did not know was he had inadvertently agreed to have Queen Esther killed, too. Of course, he had no idea she was Jewish. Letters were sent by couriers into all the king's provinces to destroy kill and annihilate all the Jews—young and old, little children, and women, in one day—on the thirteenth day of the twelfth month, (Adar) and plunder their possessions.

A copy of the document was to be issued as law in every province, published for all people so they could be ready for that day. How evil and wicked Haman's plan was! When Mordecai saw it, he was greatly troubled, and when Queen Esther heard, she was deeply distressed.

Mordecai told Esther to go before King Ahasuerus and plead with him to save her people. She knew it was against the law to go in the inner court before the king without being called, and if she did, she could be put to death. Mordecai admonished Queen Esther, saying, "For if you remain completely silent at this time, relief and deliverance will arise for the Jews from another place, but you and your father's house will perish. Yet who knows whether you have come to the kingdom for such a time as this?" (4:14).

Mordecai was saying God could save His people in many ways; God could use anyone, but He might have put Esther in that position for that very reason. Sometimes, God has a special job for us that will give us a position of authority that can be used by Him or allows us to share our faith with those around us. God will put us in the right place at the right time, just like He did for Esther.

Are you in a place where God wants to use you? to make a difference, even in one person's life, so he or she doesn't perish? In what job have you been placed? What friends or family members don't know Jesus? Are there people who need you to bring them the story of the cross to save them from eternal death? Will you share your relationship with God to save them from the wicked hand of the enemy? Esther risked her life to save a generation from perishing. Are you willing to risk your reputation and what others may think of you to share Jesus with them?

Esther's character was developed over time; she had allowed herself to be trained by the trials in her life. These produced a strong character. Now she is facing another test. Will she do the right thing in a time of adversity? I'm sure she felt the intense heat of the situation she was experiencing, but she emerged as pure gold.

"In this you greatly rejoice, though now for a little while, if need be, you have been grieved by various trials, that the genuineness of your faith, *being* much more precious than gold that perishes, though it is tested by fire, may be found to praise, honor, and glory at the revelation of Jesus Christ" (1 Peter 1:6, 7).

Just like gold is purified through the refining process in the fire, so the challenges and trials of Esther's life enabled God to prepare her for such a time as this. The trials that strengthened her character would serve her now in one of the most difficult times of her life. Her character helped her do the right thing, but her faith allowed her to take the action that was needed—an action motivated by love. Esther took a brave step of faith, as a woman of God, and He used her mightily for His glory. Esther did not waver in the face of adversity because she knew God was bigger than her situation was.

How did Esther do what God had prepared for her? She did so by overcoming her fear through the strength of Christ. "There is no fear in love; but perfect love casts out fear" (1 John 4:18). If you have ever wondered if you are doing the right thing, ask yourself, 'What is my motive?' Esther's action was motivated by love for others, and God's love moved in her heart so strongly that she chose to do what was right, but not before she fasted and prayed and had others join her.

Esther knew the severity of what she was facing. "For the love of Christ compels us" (2 Cor. 5:14). There is "a time to keep silence, and a time to speak" (Eccles. 3:7). Esther wanted to remain silent, but she couldn't. The love of God compelled her so strongly that she decided she couldn't live with herself if she kept quiet.

Esther was a queen and knew that before she could go into the inner court, she had to put on her royal robes. Sometimes, I think we need to remember who we are in Christ. Esther knew who she was. Have you forgotten whose you are and what you are in Christ? You are a daughter of the King—His queen. You are victorious. You are an overcomer; you are not defeated.

Some of us have forgotten to put on our royal robes. We have some royal clothes—not those of defeat and despair, but of victory and strength. "She is clothed with strength and dignity" (Prov. 31:25, NIV). Esther didn't put on her own clothes; she put on her royal robes. She knew who she was in the Lord. Her strength and confidence were in Him. She fasted; she prayed; she put her faith in God, and He reminded her who she was and what she was in Him. Esther claimed the victory because God wins every time!

Remember who you are in Christ. Don't search for your self-esteem or self-worth in what others say or think, but find your value in who God says you are. You are a daughter of the King. You need to see yourself as God sees you. He sees you complete and beautiful in Him. He sees you redeemed, transformed, and perfect through His love. You are beautiful, just how He made you.

What happened after Queen Esther fasted and put on her royal robes? "Now it happened on the third day that Esther put on her royal robes and stood in the inner court of the king's palace" (Esther 5:1). She found favor with the king. She could have been put to death for going against the law by entering his inner court without being called, but the king said he will grant Esther's request—up to half his kingdom! Queen Esther simply asked for the king and Haman to go to a banquet she had prepared for them, and the king granted her request. She wanted to show King Ahasuerus the evil plan Haman had plotted against the Jews.

Esther found her shelter of protection in God. "You are my hiding place and my shield; I hope in your word" (Ps. 119:114). Her shield of faith protected her. "Above all, taking the shield of faith with which you will be able to quench all the fiery darts of the wicked one" (Eph. 6:16).

As we continue, we will see the wisdom God gave Esther through her time of fasting to outsmart the enemy, Haman. In chapter 7, the king and Haman go to the banquet that Queen Esther had prepared. "And on the second day, at the banquet of wine, the king again said to Esther, 'What is your petition, Queen Esther? It shall be granted to you. And what is your request, up to half the kingdom? It shall be done!'" (verse 2).

Esther could have asked for up to half the kingdom, but she didn't. She used her position, not for selfish or evil ambition, but for good—for God's glory. Now we see she revealed her nationality as a Jew.

> Esther answered and said, "If I have found favor in your sight, O king, and if it pleases the king, let my life be given me at my petition, and my people at my request. For we have been sold, my people and I, to be destroyed, to be killed, and to be annihilated. Had we been sold as male and female slaves, I would have held my tongue, although the enemy could never compensate for the king's loss." (Esther 7:3, 4)

King Ahasuerus asked who would do such a thing. Her finger outstretched across the table, Esther pointed at Haman. The king was filled with wrath and left the room. Haman's plan would've killed the queen, the woman he loved. When he had calmed himself, Ahasuerus came back into the room and immediately dispatched his guards to take care of Haman.

"Now Esther spoke again to the king, fell down at his feet, and implored him with tears to counteract the evil of Haman the Agagite, and the scheme which he had devised against the Jews" (8:3). Later, she asked the king to revoke the letters Haman had devised. Queen Esther found favor with the king and used the very position God allowed her to fill to save the Jews. Ahasuerus gave her his signet ring to write a decree that no one could reverse. Esther fulfilled God's call for her life!

Throughout the book of Esther, we see the love and favor the king had for her. "The king loved Esther more than all the other women, and she obtained grace and favor in his sight more than all the virgins; so he set the royal crown upon her head and made her queen" (2:17). It reminds me of the deep love God, our King, has for each one of us. We find grace, favor, and love in His eyes, and one day soon, God will place a crown on each of our heads.

Remember, you belong to the King; therefore, you are a queen—His queen—one of a kind; uniquely, divinely made; a mosaic masterpiece. You are as unique as is a fingerprint—no two are the same. You have different gifts and talents compared to anyone else, so go ahead and be who God created you to be.

Maybe, because of what you have experienced, you don't feel like a queen—your crown is dashed in pieces on the ground. You may have been abused physically, mentally, emotionally, or sexually, but God takes all the broken pieces—yes, even these pieces—and makes a masterpiece—a mosaic work of art. He takes the broken pieces of your life and makes something so beautiful—so unique—different from anyone else. He will heal you and use those pieces for His glory. God's love runs deeper than any scar can.

> Maybe, because of what you have experienced, you don't feel like a queen — your crown is dashed in pieces on the ground. You may have been abused physically, mentally, emotionally, or sexually, but God takes all the broken pieces — yes, even these pieces — and makes a masterpiece.

Are you willing to give these pieces to God? He can be trusted. Allow Him to take them and carefully place them in the center of His will. Give every broken piece to God because He is kind, loving, and trustworthy. He sees you through the eyes of His love. He sees you as perfect—perfectly loved by Him.

Has your crown fallen off because of hurt? Has your crown been trampled by insults? Let God's love brush it off and make the diamonds sparkle. You are victorious. Clean off the mud of self-doubt and fear and let the rubies shine. Be you! Don't let anyone stop you from being the woman God intended you to be. Have you forgotten you are a child of the King? Put that crown back on. Dust off the dirt and let the gem of who you are shine through.

Go ahead, girl! Say it! "God is my King. I am one of a kind and deeply loved. I can do all things through Christ who strengthens me." God has paid a price for you. He has gone the distance no one else will go for you. His love doesn't give up on you.

> "Blessed is the woman who perseveres under trial,
> Because when she has stood the test,
> she will receive the crown of life that
> God has promised to those who love him."
> James 1:12 (NIV)

Relevant Lessons from Esther's Life

- **Trials and testing are not easy.** These times are difficult, but as we give them to God and allow Him to have His perfect way in us, the end result is beautiful. "My brethren, count it all joy when you fall into various trials, knowing that the testing of your faith produces patience. But let patience have its perfect work, that you may be perfect and complete, lacking nothing" (James 1:2).

- When we go through times of testing, it will often cause us to fall on our knees in prayer and call out to God. We realize we can't do it on our own, and as our faith is tested, we see the power of God. "I will bring the one-third through the fire, Will refine them as silver is refined, And test them as gold is tested. They will call on My name, And I will answer them. I will say, 'This is My people'; And each one will say, 'The Lord is my God'" (Zech. 13:9).

- **Be wise and listen to godly advice.** In listening to godly advice and instruction, you will become even wiser.

- "Give instruction to a wise man, and he will be still wiser; Teach a just man, and he will increase in learning" (Prov. 9:9).

- "He who walks with wise men will be wise, But the companion of fools will be destroyed" (13:20).

- "Without counsel, plans go awry, But in the multitude of counselors they are established" (15:22).

- **Be motivated by love.** True love comes from God, so as Esther surrendered her position to God, He motivated her by His love. Let the love of Christ compel you. Let His love be the wind in your sails.

- **Fasting and prayer are powerful.** Before going into spiritual battle, fast and pray. Esther knew she couldn't win the battle on her own. She knew the victory would be won by the Lord. She spent time in prayer and fasting and had others pray and fast with her.

- "For we do not wrestle against flesh and blood, but against principalities, against powers, against the rulers of the darkness of this age, against spiritual hosts of wickedness in the heavenly places" (Eph. 6:12).

- "And Jehoshaphat feared, and set himself to seek the LORD, and proclaimed a fast throughout all Judah.... And [the Spirit of the LORD] said, 'Listen, all you of Judah and you inhabitants of Jerusalem, and you, King Jehoshaphat! Thus says the LORD to you: "Do not be afraid nor dismayed because of this great multitude, for the battle *is* not yours, but God's"'" (2 Chron. 20:3, 15).

- Rely on God and put on your shield of faith. You don't know what life has in store for you, but God does. He knows His plans for you. He knows your makeup—how He has uniquely created you—and where He can use you for mighty things, if you are willing.

- Step out in faith by overcoming doubt and fear—by knowing who you are in Christ. Remember, God has created you to be you. He has given you unique gifts and talents to be used by Him. If you don't believe you can, the Holy Spirit equips you with power. You can do all things through Him (see Phil. 4:13).

- God has created you to move mountains—to walk by faith, not by sight. He has plans for your life and will equip you for everything He calls you to do. Don't let fear and doubt hold You back. You are one of a kind, so be you and let God's love shine through you!

Reflection Questions

God used the pain and trials Esther had experienced to refine her character. Are you allowing God to use the trials in your life to produce His character—love, patience, goodness, kindness, and self-control?

As a young woman, Esther lost both parents, but she learned to trust a godly mentor. Godly mentors are important. Is there someone God has placed in your life to help you? or is there someone God would like for you to mentor?

Esther learned to trust God. She knew she couldn't rely on her own strength. Is there an area in your life in which you know you can't excel without His help? Are you willing to fast and pray to see God's power move through you?

Is there a Bible verse from this study that has helped you that you would like to share? Write it here.

Can you see how God has taken the pieces of your life to mold you into a woman He can employ for His benevolent purposes?

Are you willing to give God all the pieces, even the ones that have caused you hurt, so He can heal you and use them for His glory?

Remember, you are deeply loved by God, the One who cares for you.

TEACH Services, Inc.
PUBLISHING

We invite you to view the complete
selection of titles we publish at:
www.TEACHServices.com

We encourage you to write us
with your thoughts about this,
or any other book we publish at:
info@TEACHServices.com

TEACH Services' titles may be purchased in
bulk quantities for educational, fund-raising,
business, or promotional use.
bulksales@TEACHServices.com

Finally, if you are interested in seeing
your own book in print, please contact us at:
publishing@TEACHServices.com

We are happy to review your manuscript at no charge.

www.ingramcontent.com/pod-product-compliance
Lightning Source LLC
Chambersburg PA
CBHW070546170426
43200CB00011B/2574